Family *or* Friends
Blood or Water

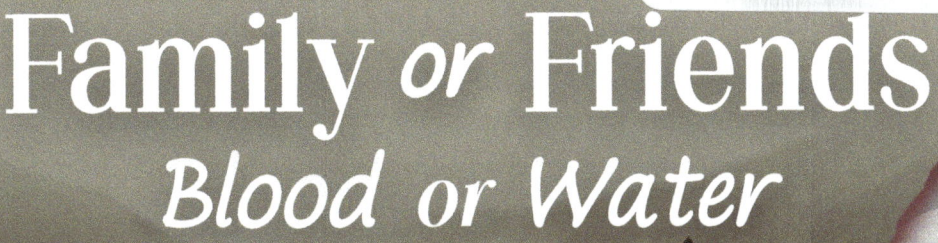

Vincent R. Petrucci

Inks and Bindings
888-290-5218
www.inksandbindings.com
orders@inksandbindings.com

Contents

This book is dedicated to my immediate family

Thank you for such wonderful life

It did not rain everyday

Family or Friends
Blood or Water

T he sun was warm that autumn day. It appeared to be an Indian Summer, the sky was a bit hazy, and the water in the swimming pool was warm though mid-October. The entire family was out messing around spending time together cleaning the yard. There was conversation amongst each other. Daisy Jane felt good, this was not the norm. There were many times the family exhibited Disarray.

Daisy Jane was taking some college classes yet her mind was always looking for adventure, she had the ability to become whatever she wanted. The remainder of her time was spent working at small Boutiques. Daisy had been in a fashion school in San Francisco California. Her parents were kind and wanted to see their daughter flourish. They had sent Daisy to study fashion, yet Daisy was not grounded at this time in her life. Daisy was ready to pursue her dream of having her own line of clothes however school was not happening.

Daisy coming from Italian American family had traveled to visit family in Europe. Rome, Milan Paris always stuck in her mind. Different attire then America. Daisy always imagined her own Brand. Flowers by Daisy Jane that was what she wanted her line to be called. Daisy Jane loved the outdoors and nature. She enjoyed small animals, in fact she had many pets, dogs, birds and ducks, to a black horse. Always out riding her beautiful smoky with her animal friends following her. Friends would say, there is DJ out with her family in the pastures with the white clover flowers at her feet.. It seemed Daisy was content, her favorite friend Scarlett would come over they would get lost riding that black horse, bareback DJ Leading and Scarlett to her back smoking an occasional cigarette or sweet J. Not a care.

JC

Daisy Jane preparing awaiting Scarlett to pick her up for class that Tuesday morning, driving into the city Daisy lit up a J, hey DJ said to Scarlett we have an exam today are you ready. Scarlett gazed over to her right pulled her dark shades down and lifted up 2 copies of the exam. So nice DJ thought. Scarlett gave one to DJ. Now DJ's anxiety was over, the exam would be uncomplicated.. Daisy knew it was not right, however her mind was not into to school, her days in high school were low key. College took discipline. DJ was into adventure not studying. Post the exam Scarlett was waiting for Daisy. How did you do. Answered all the questions. The next week in class the Professor handed out all the students' exams. DJ and Scarlett did not receive their exam, the teacher called them up after class.

Mr. R greeted the two, I see the exams you took are really the same. You both received 93 percent the highest in the class. You missed the same questions. It is strange your written-out answers are near exact of one another. Mr. R. was puzzled a small physical stature gentleman with a strong Eastern Indian Accent. He was a very fair professor and kind.

Please realize your life is just starting and I want you to be successful. Try to grasp the act of dishonestly is not allowed in higher education and in fact in any school. Please take this in consideration for our next exam in 2 weeks.

DJ and Scarlett walked out of the classroom, they looked at each other back in Scarlett's car that nice clean Blue Mustang, Hey School is just not for me DJ said to Scarlett, yes I agree.

I am out I am not coming back. DJ knew her family would not want this, however she was hurting herself doing something that she was always fighting. DJ was into riding smoky. The outdoors was where her heart was. The evenings back in her room would be drawing and designing her clothing line. Flowers her brand name. . Daisy was slim with long legs. She liked the look, blue jeans with the brand name stamped on the back Flowers by DJ. Daisy thought it had a nice feel.. I can market that.

Weekend

D aisy was having a difficult time on explaining to her parents that college was just not her. Sunday would be the day during the afternoon lunch, Daisy was a bit nervous however was able to disclose to her parents that she was out of her Junior college classes. I am not ready at 19-years old to commit to studies.

DJ's father was understanding He was strict yet fair. Daisy's mother was pressing her on what will you do. Daisy stated she had an interview at one of the fast-food restaurants in the small city. They hired me. All at the table that sunny afternoon were happy for DJ. Let's go swimming after lunch, then we can visit your grandparents. DJ was close with her grandmother. She enjoyed assisting her cooking and mending clothes by hand. Family was precious for DJ.

Job

Daisy Jane's first week at her job went well, Scarlett also was hired. DJ was content, has money and was happy to be with her best friend. DJ continued to work on her clothing line when not at her fast-foods job.

DJ's grandmother had an old sewing Machine and Daisy would always watch her mend clothes. DJ new how to use the machine, her Grandmother taught her how to sew buttons on shirts.

DJ started to make alterations to her blue jeans. Her brand name flowers by DJ was on the back right pocket. It was bright yellow Stamp made out of leather. The Name Flowers was in Dark black. It stood out. Daisy was proud of her Style. Straight blue jeans loose fitting.

DJ thought it's nice for the spring and summer. DJ's parents were also content. Daisy was a bit rebellious and the family wanted her to stay busy with work and her interest in sewing.

Scarlett would come by the house and visit with DJ. Her parents liked Scarlett, yet knew when the 2 young adults were together they deviated from the norm.

Hey Letty, Scarlett's nickname given to her by DJ. Let's take Smoky out for a walk.. Scarlett enjoyed going bareback riding as well.

Let's go out to the pasture with the small white flowers DJ stated to Scarlett.. Smoky was a gentle black horse around 5 years old and height was 15 hands, thus average size horse.

Smoky liked to gallop. Both teens enjoyed to be lost in the huge pasture land smoking a Dobbie and talking about life sad and happy times.

DJ what do you think about driving down to Mexico. Wow thought DJ… I never really been, so I don't know, yet I would like to experience that. Sure we could take my car, the light blue mustang daddy had bought Letty the car used, however it was very clean with air conditioning working and a nice 8 track stereo system.

DJ thought about her family how all was going well. Her job was fun and plus little extra money for gas in her Green and white Chevrolet. It was an old truck, had lots of power, the manual transmission was what DJ had learned to drive when she was a young girl. Her father taught her. DJ was close with her parents, moreover respected them. Daisy thoughts however as of late were preoccupied with taking a ride down the California coast with Letty, how exciting.

Not a care

That afternoon DJ and Scarlett working at the fast food's Drive in talked about what they wanted to do. Letty mentioned she had saved few dollars enough to get down to Baja California. I want to visit Santa Barbara explained DJ. Scarlett was in, yes we can visit Tommy and Rhea. These were friends from high school and were attending College.

Letty was an only child, her parents gave her whatever she wanted. Her father was a city cop that enjoyed a nice strong drink. Her mother was a free-spirited individual. The family tight knit seemed to always be enjoying life. DJ fit right in. Letty was tall, she had long legs that were always tanned. Her Sandy blonde hair always neat and shinning. Letty loved her dark red lipstick and painted toe nails to match.

DJ off days away from work were spent at Grandma's. They had good conversation and Daisy was a good student with grandma teaching her about life.

Daisy Jane enjoyed helping grandma make home-made pies and sewing clothes, DJ appeared to be content around her family, yet always wanted to pursue her dream of Flowers her clothing line. Grandma, DJ would say one day I will have Scarlett modeling my casual clothing line flowers by Daisy Jane. Letty with a perfect body long legs and her bottom so round. She could be in Paris Milan and or New York. I love Letty grandma.

Grandmother would just listen to her. Yes honey replied grandmother, you can do whatever your heart desires. Your family adores you and is supported in your future. DJ, yes grandma I love you. Keep your hopes high honey.

Scarlett Yes DJ calling her, can I come over and go swimming, sure. Let's talk about that drive down the California coast to Mexico.

Letty's mother greeted DJ at the front door, Scarlett is in the back yard. She is tanning. Both young women enjoyed the nice warm sun on that October day. How are you Scarlett, I am well worked yesterday. I had a good day. Have you seen Frankie, no he is doing his own thing lately replied Scarlett. I enjoy his company yet that is it. You DJ have you interacted with your man. No DJ stated. I have been with grandma. How is your brother DJ, oh Carlos. Yes silly your only brother.

He is well, you know we have a good relationship and hang out at times. Carlos is like me Letty he enjoys adventure and getting lost in the moment. Our family is doing well now no issues, the sandwich business is expanding. Carlos has his own route and seems to like the idea of being on his own.

The mornings start early preparing Sandwiches then Carlos makes his deliveries. I am happy for him.

So Letty let's plan our trip. Yes sure Daisy, however you absolutely sure you want to leave now. It appears your family is doing well. It was last month that there was all the Chaos. I understand Letty no I am not so certain. Family is so special you, you're my rock Letty, we can talk about anything replied Daisy. The two 19 yr old embraced and shed a tear. Your family is awesome. They really support you DJ. Yes Grandma also mentioned. I can do whatever I want. Family is there.

Yes Letty I feel sometimes I am influenced by my friends at times, especially you Scarlett. 19 yrs old high-spirited DJ always wanted to move forward and live her dream Flowers by DJ her own clothing line. Well Scarlett the modeling school in San Francisco, I was home sick, college you understand. Yes I do DJ. Ok so next week Is Halloween, leave from my house on the day before. Oct 30. My mother will be at the salon. My father working.

Drive

DJ arrived early. What did you say to your family DJ, they think I have work today. I told my mom I was staying with you tonight.

The day was sunny that beautiful October morning. Brisk, breezing. DJ mentioned to Letty you look so sexy in the Yellow tube top, your nipples are hard. Yes DJ, my mother gave me those. DJ dressed in her casual blue jeans. She had sewed the Leather Brand bright yellow on the back right pocket Flowers By Daisy Jane. Wow DJ.

You look so beautiful. You will be successful in your clothing line Flowers by DJ.. Yes I was just experimenting with this pair. yours are in my suit case. Oh you brought a suitcase. I just brought my back pack stated Letty. Sounds cool.

Hit this Letty, as Scarlet was driving down 145 south toward the California coast. We go through Kerman, then pass the five points road. DJ looked at Scarlett, we are on our way. I feel Happy this morning Oct 30.

DJ we are almost at the split. Let's go straight towards Morro Bay. I like that place. My father climbed the Morro Bay Rock when he Attending San Luis Cal Poly.

Yes there is a nice place to eat there, stated Daisy, my mother loves the spot. What is the name DJ, inquired Letty. Breakers. , yes Letty. Do not worry just park up the road a bit. There is a small park space up the Hill.

This is awesome Letty, looking out over the Bay towards Morro Rock. Wow your father climbed that. It so huge. Yes, it's off limits now stated Daisy Jane.

I want shrimp, those really fancy type with the red sauce and lots of lemon. DJ reminiscing, I have been coming here for so many yrs as a young child. My father had always attended conferences at Cal

Poly. The family would stay a few days. Peggy Louise enjoyed it here. I can just see her now Smoking a cigarette with that red lipstick on. The smoke made me feel bad.

Your mother had a cute name. I guess. She named me Daisy Jane. I love your name DJ mentioned Scarlett. Do you have a middle name Letty. You never told me.. well I guess I can tell you. Please do please.. Mary. Scarlett Mary, ahhh really. Wow Letty looking at DJ.

It is beautiful. Letty looking over at DJ smiling with her sexy small eyes. DJ I want what you are getting yes Shrimp.

Yes sure. The two enjoyed the fresh shrimp cocktail with all the red sauce and lemons.. Letty how was that, so good stated Letty. What do you think about some clam chowder. Yes let's order a small bowl.

This is so fun Letty. I am enjoying time with you. You are my friend yet you feel like family we never have commotion. Well DJ families are like that. Your family wants the best for you.

Look at that seagull, it just went face first in the ocean and caught a fish.. So free the bird is. I feel like a bird today free Letty.

Scarlett, I am going to the CR. Meet you outside. I will pay. Scarlet finishing her soup, glanced up at DJ yes sure.

Let's go Letty, DJ seemed in a hurry, why so fast. Oh well I guess they call that dine and dash. DJ you are like a free bird. Just flying away. Start the car, here put on this blue scarf Letty. It matches your car. Go hurry DJ motioned to Letty, you do not look so conspicuous with that Italian scarf on covering your glowing hair.

This is such a beautiful day I want to capture it forever, the two 19 yrs old driving down 101 south, Scarlett did you enjoy our peaceful lunch. What are you crazy DJ, why did you do that Leave without paying. I was, was just living in the moment..

Are you ok Letty, Certainly DJ. I want to get some Candy and gum. You want to drive DJ, I will go in the liquor store and buy a couple items cigarettes and a coke. Sure, why are you pulling to the side.

Letty entered the store. DJ had noticed Letty had taken off the Italian scarf. It was now around her face covering it completely.

My god what is she doing thought DJ. Go What happen Letty?. I just did a dine and dash at the liquor store.

Oh really DJ was short of words. Yes why, well I thought if you can do that at the Breakers, then why not I want to be exactly like you DJ.

DJ now cruising down 101 south on that beautiful October day.

Solvang

D J yes Letty it's almost 5 PM the sun is setting, stop at the next turnout and we can trip watch the sun set. Sure, Letty had rolled some sweet Thai stick.

Amazing day DJ, Frankie turned me on to this. Hit it. DJ inhaled had in and then started coughing and laughing allowing the sweet smoke to come out of her cute lips.

What the fuck did you do at the Liquor Store. Reds? Yes is that the name of place you said you Dined and dash. No not really like that DJ stated Letty. I put that Beautiful Blue Italian Scarf over my face Held my brush in my coat pocket and ordered the old man behind the counter to give me all his money, he thought I had a gun.

What the fuck, yes I did. Then I saw him go to the phone. I grabbed the gum candy and cigarettes and split.

Amazing Letty, DJ continued to laugh. No care. Free as the seagull at the breakers diving for fish.

Hey Daisy Jane, both teens now feeling no pain laughing and embracing each other sitting next to each looking out at the Sunset. I am sorry for what I did back there at Reds. Not a thing, Letty replied DJ.

This is our trip DJ stated to Letty and I am enjoying it. Let's drive into Solvang DJ, yes we can. Both had been there in the past with their families.

What do you feel, I am thinking of a nice hot shower and sleeping DJ. Flyers is a Motel at the end of the main street.

I have an idea DJ. We park across the street at the supermarket, walk across the main street. Letty Look there is the maid's cart. Ok look the keys. You have your backpack Letty, Grab the keys

Look the room is facing opposite the managers office. No one is around Letty, DJ took the keys from Letty and open Room I.

Get in the shower and enjoy yourself. I am going to roll a bud. Oh my, what a feeling DJ the water feels like Heaven. Just hold me tight all the time Letty. I am happy with you, what about your family DJ well I said I was staying the night with you, yes I told my Mother I was staying with you tonight DJ.

Let's sleep Letty, this is a nice twin bed and we can cuddle all night. Yes My dearest Daisy Jane, the fashion designer.

Letty get up, look the sun is up and its warm. The Indian summer is sticking around. Today is Oct 31. Happy Halloween DJ, I brought this simple cat eye mask. I have a blue one and I Have red one for you.

The maid, oh stated Letty put the keys back. Ask her if we can have some coffee, she is smiling at us. Is there any coffee, asked Letty. Follow the small path to the office area they are serving breakfast and coffee.

DJ follow me, Look let's just blend in. You are so smart Letty explained DJ you always do the right thing and make good decisions. Seriously, DJ right choices. We just came down 101 south on a coastal spree.

Forget about it Letty, this is better than work.

Get the car, put on your red mask. Happy Halloween. Twist one of those beautiful Thai sticks. Vandenberg, ahh yes I came here 10 years ago with my 6th grade class. We drove all night in the school bus and it was so cold.

We watched a rocket launch, it was fantastic. The noise was extremely scary. Head south down the highway 1. Look Letty they say this is one of the most beautiful coastline Highway 1.

I am with you DJ. My mother always talks about the white caps. Love my mother Letty, she is real. Not educated like my father, however has good common sense and a great heart.

I really feel she loves Carlos more them me. DJ he is the younger child. Why are you crying DJ, I am ok. You're not alone DJ I am here for you. I love you DJ I love you Letty.

When we were young, we lived a life without any doubt. Now I feel it's changing. It is life DJ changes happen We must learn to pivot. I feel pain at times. Just be over it. Do not cry. You look so cute with those tears falling down your face with the cat yes mask.

Honeymoon

Tommy and Rhea are living together Letty, I have Rhea's address. Why not stop and say hello. Halloween evening should be a treat or perhaps a trick.

Take the State Street exit Letty, this avenue is cool so many different sites. Galleries and Restaurant.

Look there is Garretts. That is old spot Letty mentioned DJ, I have eaten here with my family.. They have great breakfast. Hey DJ, no more crazy today. It fine. Both 19 yrs old with their cat eyes mask.

Park, Letty. Let's walk down to the Wharf. Roll a doobie. Let's stroll. Look DJ they all are on skates. We can rent a pair, 1.25 for two hours.

Such a sweet day. Halloween 1979. I will remember this day forever DJ. This really beats roller skating at The High School.. Yes yet there something special about yelling through the quarters.. and smoking on campus Sunday's afternoon. Yes Letty.. I guess.

Let's skate down towards the art Museum. Ok DJ nothing out of the normal no.. I wish we had a camera to capture some of the events and save for ever. I am just dreaming said Letty.

Tommy and Rhea are staying out near the University Letty, yes I love watching all these folks in costumes. It not even night. Wild, that appears to be a M and M, she is with a beautiful lady all dressed up like a Prostitute chewing that gum with her short skirt. What if Tommy and Rhea are in class, Scarlett? Well, would you show up to the address. They are cool and would you say hello. If they're not home, we can leave a note.

My parents came here on their Honeymoon did you know that Letty?

Did you know they eloped, went to Vegas got married. My father's roommate at college and best friend was his best man.

My Nonno was not in favor of my father marrying a woman from the south. He wanted him to be with an Italian woman. I guess they were in deep love. Been together ever since. Santa Barbara is where they spent their Honeymoon.

My mother always talks about the Santa Barbara Inn, beautiful and the flowers and ocean views. My mother coming from the south was not exposed to ocean like we have in California. I guess they stayed a few days and enjoyed what newlyweds do.

My mother was so special in my eyes. She was not really a dreamer like me. She enjoyed simple things in life like Ice tea ice and Corn bread. Me Letty, I want to see flowers by DJ on billboards in Down town San Francisco. It will happen DJ, replied Letty. Your mother just thought different.

Isla Vista

136

Tall street

That is the apartment complex.

They are in A, wow looks to be modern apartments, yes the family has little money. Rhea's Grandfather, she stated assisted them.

My gosh so many Bikes coming and going. All these students.. Tommy told me everyone has bikes. Look there are 2 there Letty, no DJ no more of the crazy, please.

Well appears they are not around. I mentioned to Rhea we might come by sometimes, yet that was months ago.

Look inside that apartment DJ, what that nice camera. Hey DJ the door is open. Ok so what are you saying. Don't do this CRAZY, you just reminded me.

Come on DJ look at this place all the Camera equipment, must be into Photography. Beautiful Ocean shots.

Let's get out of here Letty, yes sure. I will use their bathroom. What, Go get the Car DJ. Do not touch that Camera.

I was hoping to visit with Tommy and Rhea, next time DJ meet you at the car.

Hey Letty, yes DJ let's rent bike and ride down around the small town.

Temptation

DJ went out to start the car. Letty knowing better. However walked into the neighbors of Tommy and Rhea's apartment.

Letty what took you so long. I just need to Use the CR, oh what you have in your purse? Oh no DJ was like that is so awesome of a camera. Yes looks like a real professional type with that long zoom Lens.

How do you know about cameras Letty ask DJ, wow you know I studied Photography in high School. Both teens started to look at each and laugh. Mrs. Listien class.. You are doing the Crazy Letty again.

DJ I want to remember these moments. Nobody was around. The apartment next to Tommy and Rheas was open. So many nice items. So many cameras.

They won't even miss it Ok whatever you say Letty.

Drive south down 101 DJ We can take some crazy pictures of the free seagulls and those white caps your mother loves.

A great idea thought DJ.

Park

S top at the State Park DJ, El Capitan. We can just trip take photographs and burn a sweet one. You know Letty I feel the best has not yet come for both of us. . Seriously I agree DJ.

Letty look at that black crow. It appears so angry from atop the tree. It just won't stop crowing. It appears to be telling us something.

Yes Both girls smiling at each other weird Halloween and the Black Crow JUST WONT STOP. Maybe he does not like our cat eye masks.

Letty let's climb that small hill and look over the beach, there is a tree we can lay down underneath.

Wow such a beautiful breeze, look at the white caps DJ I am getting some beautiful pictures.

I will close my eyes Letty just take a nap sun starting to set in the west on this Indian summer afternoon in southern California... Wow I don't want sleep at all DJ.

Scarlett was awoken by two young Bicycle cops saying looks like them, DJ wake up.

Daisy Jane was staring at Scarlett, The Cops not much older than DJ and Scarlett, what are you young ladies doing here.

Just tripping watching the ocean Officers Letty mentioned. We have a report that a car matching your make model and license plate number was spotted at few establishments along the highway one freeway. One gentleman at Reds stated he was held up by gun point, damn officer wish we could assist, Letty stated. We are just visiting some friends down here in Santa Barbara. Young cops went on the say one Blonde-haired young woman with a blue scarf was seen driving away from the liquor store heading south on Highway 1.

The cops ask the two to come down to the police station. Letty I guess we have no choice. We do Letty and DJ walking towards their car with the officers behind them,. Do not say anything DJ just tell them you want to make a phone call to your family.

They are guessing, yes however we have the camera, why did you take that DJ looking at Letty in disgust.

It's ok DJ stated Letty. We still have each other. 19 and free Letty explained. Your family loves you and you will have your clothing line someday.

What do you say DJ family or friends. Who makes you happiest That is all I have to say..